*Cinebook* recounts

# Battle of Britain (1940)

**Written by: Bernard ASSO**
**Illustrated by: Francis BERGESE**

**Colour work: F.B.**

9th **CINEBOOK**
The 9th Art Publisher

Spring 1940... From the 15th of May, the Third Reich forces streamed into the northwest of France, after pushing through Sedan. France crumbled within 35 days. After having made their position for peace absolutely clear, they were dazed, surprised and defeated with no time to react. The Germans pressed their advantage and trapped the British Expeditionary Corps in the "Dunkirk Pocket." But an unusual hesitation from the German Army allowed Her Majesty's forces time to escape back to England. From then on, faced with a victorious Reich, there wasn't much hope left... The fate of the world rested on the shoulders of a handful of men: the pilots of the R.A.F.

Original title: La bataille d'Angleterre

Original edition: © Editions du Lombard (Dargaud-Lombard SA) 2003
by F. Bergèse et B. Asso
www.lelombard.com

English translation: © 2007 Cinebook Ltd

Translator: Luke Spear
Lettering and text layout: Imadjinn sarl
Printed in Spain by Just Colour Graphic

This edition first published in Great Britain in 2010 by
Cinebook Ltd
56 Beech Avenue
Canterbury, Kent
CT4 7TA
www.cinebook.com

A CIP catalogue record for this book is available from the British Library

ISBN 978-1-84918-025-2

9th CINEBOOK
The 9th Art Publisher

DUNKIRK, 3RD JUNE 1940. THE EVACUATION OF BRITISH TROOPS BEGAN ON THE 26TH OF MAY. THE ROYAL AIR FORCE STRUGGLED TO CONTAIN THE LUFTWAFFE ASSAULTS...

J.H. COLBY, FLYING OFFICER, WAS SHOT DOWN OVER THE BEACHES...

By Jove!

Sir! Are you hurt?

No, I'm all right, thank you! I have to get back to my squadron*...

*ATTACK GROUP

3

LATER...

The Krauts own the skies! But where's the Allied response?

Yes... it's atrocious! We're fighting one against a hundred!

May God protect England!

God's already helping... Fighter Command has only been able to provide 200 fighters against the whole Luftwaffe!

And the evacuation goes on all the same!

AT THAT MOMENT, IN LONDON, THE MAIN WARTIME LEADERS ASSEMBLED. AIR CHIEF MARSHAL DOWDING HAD JUST ARRIVED...

So, gentlemen, what's happening?

My concerns were justified... The battle in Europe has caused us heavy losses: 959 planes, 477 of them fighters!... Since the War Cabinet got behind my viewpoint, we've been able to conserve the majority of our defence fighters... but isn't it too late now!?

Churchill

Lord Beaverbrook

Dowding

Indeed, since September 1939, Marshal Dowding had foreseen a catastrophe. On the 15th of May 1940, he asked the Air Minister to not send planes to France so that they could conserve as many as possible to ensure the defence of the island. The War Cabinet didn't accept his point of view until the end of May 1940. This decision allowed England to save its Spitfires, which it would really need in a few months' time. This would explain the near absence of English planes over France in the spring of 1940.

What about our reserves?

We have 59 fighter squadrons of different strengths left. We have about 800 planes, of which 370 are Hurricanes and Spitfires. The rest are bombers and damaged planes. The Germans have 2600 planes, of which more than 1000 are fighters!

Our forces are split into four divisions: the 11th in the southeast to protect London, the 13th in the north, the 12th in the Midlands and the 10th, which is setting up now in the southwest. Two others are in formation to support the 12th and 13th.

COMMAND GROUPS

And what does our aeronautical production look like, Lord Beaverbrook?

At the beginning of the war we were only producing 2 Spitfires and 2 Hurricanes a day...

By Jove!

Why?

I understand your surprise... But until the 10th of May 1940, several leaders couldn't have envisaged France being defeated.

Production has been boosted to 400 planes in June alone!

Vice-Marshal Park's figures are right.

Keith Park

The 11th Group that you command will take the heaviest fire. The 12th, under Leigh-Mallory's orders, will sustain attacks from Norway and Denmark.

Our pilots are tired or inexperienced and the battle hasn't even begun yet!

Well, gentlemen, do what you must!

THE SITUATION WAS DRAMATIC, BUT...

Lucky we managed to decrypt the German code!... We will be warned of any enemy attacks. Will that be enough?...

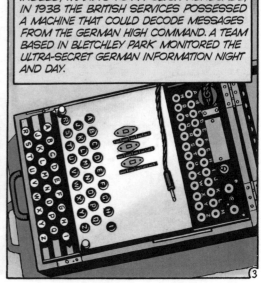

INDEED, THANKS TO A POLISH RENEGADE, IN 1938 THE BRITISH SERVICES POSSESSED A MACHINE THAT COULD DECODE MESSAGES FROM THE GERMAN HIGH COMMAND. A TEAM BASED IN BLETCHLEY PARK MONITORED THE ULTRA-SECRET GERMAN INFORMATION NIGHT AND DAY.

**18TH JUNE 1940...**

*I think that the Battle of Britain is about to start...*

*... All that's left to do is to wait for the Germans.*

*... The war continues!*

**ON THE GERMAN SIDE, THE 20TH OF JUNE 1940 AT THE WOLSSCHLUCHT MEETING...**

*A landing in England is only possible with total control of the skies!*

*My Luftwaffe will take care of that!*

Admiral Raeder    Goering

*Let's wait. I'll give England the option of peace. Let's not forget that the English are our cousins. I don't want any bombing on British territory for now...*

**A FEW DAYS LATER, THE 2ND OF JULY...**

*The Führer has decided to go ahead with preparations for an invasion: Operation Sea Lion. The Navy is preparing its files... We get the first shot! But the Führer still wants peace...*

*The Luftflotten are ready. Their orders are clear. Herr Oberst, take note: "Forbid any navigation in the Channel, destroy ports, attract the R.A.F. and destroy them"! Since Dunkirk we've been wasting time!*

**AT THAT MOMENT, THE BRITISH PILOTS WERE PREPARING FOR AN ASSAULT...**

4

The Messerschmitt totally outclasses the Hurricane!...

Not completely; if you keep swerving tightly, your opponent can't get you in his sights. On the other hand, the Spitfire has the same advantage but is a little faster.

In fact, it'd be better if the Spits attacked the German fighters and if the Hurricanes stuck to their bombers!

For the moment we don't have enough Spits!

THE GERMAN PILOTS WEREN'T WORRIED ABOUT THAT KIND OF THING YET...

Good fishing today, Oberleutnant?

Nein! Nothing biting today!

OTTO WERNER, LIEUTENANT...

Otto! How are you?

Tired!

I missed a Hurricane. He got away with a double barrel and a double loop. The boat convoy that we were attacking was spitting out hellfire!

I fought over Dunkirk. The R.A.F. pilots are no dummies! We'll have our work cut out...

5

I've got the feeling that the High Command is hesitating!

The air fights are taking place higher and higher... up to 9000 meters. But our weaponry is superior.

We'll see. Let's drink!

Prosit!

10TH JULY 1940. AT MIDDAY, THE DORNIER 17Z OF THE I/KG2 GROUP TOOK OFF FOR ENGLAND...

The Messerschmitt 109 should meet up with us...

Major Fuchs promised us the 110* too. All the English can do is try to hold out!

*BI-MOTOR ESCORT FIGHTERS

THIS WAS THE FIRST BIG ENGAGEMENT OF THE BATTLE OVER THE CHANNEL...

13ʜ31
10ʜ50
10ʜ50

London
SY 32, 74, 111
SPITFIRE    DO 17, BF 110
HURRICANE   DO17

Canterbury    SPIT.
RAID BF 109

Hastings    SY 610
SPITFIRE
CONVOY "BREAD"

AT THAT MOMENT, IN THE OPERATIONS ROOM AT FIGHTER COMMAND...

Let's focus on the enemies in Northumberland and on the Pas de Calais. They're going for the bread convoy!

Scramble! Falcons take off!

SQUADRONS 32, 74 AND 111 TOOK OFF IMMEDIATELY...

109s at 4 o'clock overhead!... Stick to him better than that, Blue 2!... Look out behind you!... 109s at 12 o'clock!...

It's getting tight up there!

Tally-ho!

I got him!

There's a concentration off the coast of Cornwall! Scramble!

IT LASTED ALL DAY. THE R.A.F. MADE 600 SORTIES AND LOST SIX PLANES. THE GERMANS LOST 13 PLANES...

Francis Bergèse

9

DESPITE ALREADY HAVING LAUNCHED HIS FIRST ATTACKS, HITLER STILL HADN'T TAKEN HIS FINAL DECISION. THE 16TH OF JULY 1940...

The Luftwaffe is keeping up the pressure on the Channel!

I've decided to prepare for an invasion of England. And, if necessary, carry it out. This will be the objective of Directive 16.

What is the Führer waiting for to take a final decision?

He has summoned the Reichstag on the 19th July... He wants peace in the west so he can wage war in the east!

22nd July 1940...

Lord Halifax has just rejected an offer for peace... The air war will intensify!

We don't deal with murderers!

Ah! Colby, I forgot! Congratulations on your promotion to Flight Lieutenant!

John was shot down because he forgot these warnings.

Come on! Have a drink on me! May luck be on our side...

KRAUTS ALWAYS IN THE SUN!
IT'S THE ONE YOU DIDN'T SEE WHO'LL TAKE YOU DOWN!
NEVER FOLLOW A HIT PLANE!

LUCK? FIGHTER COMMAND TRIED TO PUT IT ON THEIR SIDE BY ANY MEANS NECESSARY...

Our "small packets" tactic is giving good results. We should avoid any large-scale engagement... That's the trap that Goering is trying to lure us into. He's looking for a pitched battle.

But our pilots are tired. They are attacking in groups of six to 12 against 50!

I know. But I have to save the planes. We need to stay at a loss ratio of one to 2.5! Yesterday, 24th July, we lost three planes against seven for the Germans.

Vice-Marshal Leigh-Mallory thinks that Douglas Bader is right... He suggested we resort to massive interception.

There's no way! We can use the small packet tactic thanks to our radar cover.

AS SOON AS THE ATTACKERS WERE PICKED UP, THE PATROL SQUADRONS INTERCEPTED THEM, AND THEN THE REINFORCEMENTS CAME. BARON DOWDING COULD DEMONSTRATE THE EFFICIENCY OF HIS TACTIC THIS WAY, DESPITE CRITICISM.

We need pilots... We've drawn from our volunteers in France, Belgium, Poland, Czechoslovakia and elsewhere. These "amateurs" from the reserves have become veterans!

Have they lost their fun, eccentric side in the exchange?

Look! They've formed a swastika!

NOT QUITE... THE RESERVE FORCES HAD BEEN BUILT UP SINCE 1925. MEMBERS OF THE AUXILIARY FORCES, VOLUNTEERS FOR THE RESERVES, UNIVERSITY AVIATION GROUPS, THESE "AMATEURS" HAD KEPT THEIR TASTE FOR TRICKERY. SO, AT THE START OF THE WAR, SQUADRON 611...

Ha! I remember that story!

Coming back to the criticism of certain people, I would like to point out that I will not budge on this tactic, no more than I did to take from the North of England to help the South!

INDEED, THE 2ND OF AUGUST 1940, AT KARINHALL, GOERING'S RESIDENCE...

On the 30th of July, the Führer gave me the order for a total assault. It will take place around the 13th of August and will be called "Day of the Eagle!" The success of our invasion will depend on this victory.

THE PLAN FOR THIS ATTACK WAS AS FOLLOWS:

LUFTFLOTTE V: STUMPFL
LUFTFLOTTE II: KESSERLING

FIGHTERS:
BOMBERS:

PARIS

STUKA

LUFTFLOTTE III: SPERRLE

ON THE 30TH OF JULY 1940, IN BERCHTESGADEN, ADMIRAL ROEDER HAD A FEW DOUBTS...

We need total air domination! Mine sweeping to prepare for the invasion will take five weeks. I'm not sure about a full and definitive victory over the R.A.F.!

THE FIRST PHASE OF THE BATTLE BEGAN ON THE 8TH OF AUGUST...

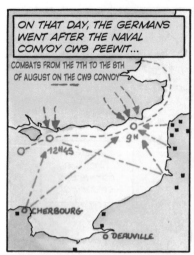

ON THAT DAY, THE GERMANS WENT AFTER THE NAVAL CONVOY CW9 PEEWIT...

COMBATS FROM THE 7TH TO THE 8TH OF AUGUST ON THE CW9 CONVOY

9H

12H45

CHERBOURG

DEAUVILLE

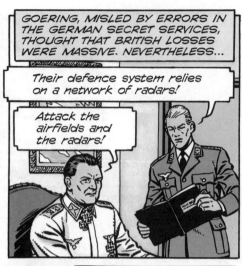

GOERING, MISLED BY ERRORS IN THE GERMAN SECRET SERVICES, THOUGHT THAT BRITISH LOSSES WERE MASSIVE. NEVERTHELESS...

Their defence system relies on a network of radars!

Attack the airfields and the radars!

12TH AUGUST 1940, IN ENGLAND...

Yesterday we shot down 38 German planes, but we lost 32 fighters.

Too many losses!

The Germans are concentrating their attacks on our radars. For now, the weather conditions are in our favour!

If they keep this up we'll not be able to hold out. We have to warn the Prime Minister.

AT THAT MOMENT...

We've intercepted a German message: Time has slipped away... Operation Day of the Eagle begins tomorrow, Sir!

Alert Dowding!

THE 13TH OF AUGUST, AT 2:30PM, MESSER-SCHMITT BF109S OF THE LUFTFLOTTE III TOOK OFF FOR THE NORTH OF ENGLAND...

ON ANOTHER BASE, AT THE SAME TIME, JU88AS OF THE K.G.54 LEFT THEIR RUNWAYS...

THE ALERT WAS GIVEN IN ENGLAND...

Formations over Southampton!

Attacks over Hampshire. Scramble! Scramble!!!

10

THE ENGLISH HUNT TOOK TO THE AIR...

My goodness! The whole Luftwaffe's out! Only Goering's missing!

Bandits at 3 o'clock! Spits attack the fighters; we'll take the bombers!... Tally ho!!!

Swine!

HOWEVER, OTTO WERNER...

You will give in!!!

AT THE LAST MINUTE THE SPIT-FIRE PILOT DID A NOSE-DIVE TO AVOID COLLISION, AND THEN...

OVER THE CLIFFS OF DOVER, THERE WAS NO LACK OF SPECTATORS...

THE BATTLE CONTINUED INTO THE NIGHT. THE LUFTWAFFE *SENT OUT 1484 PLANES, LOST 45 PLANES AND ONLY TOOK DOWN 13 R.A.F. FIGHTERS*. IT WAS A BLACK TUESDAY FOR THE LUFTWAFFE...

*Dear listeners... A victory!... The 609th Squadron has shot down 13 Stuka in 13 minutes!*

*Leigh-Mallory's 12th group have to support me!*

*No! The Germans are waiting for us to weaken the northern front!*

INDEED, THE 15TH OF AUGUST 1940, THE LUFTFLOTTE V OF GENERAL OBERST STUMPFF, BASED IN NORWAY AND DENMARK, WENT ON THE OFFENSIVE...

*Targets: Dishforth, Usworth, Middlesbrough, Newcastle, Sunderland...*

12

THE 15ᵀᴴ OF AUGUST 1940, AT MIDDAY, GERMAN BOMBERS SPREAD OUT BETWEEN 3500 AND 5500 METRES. ABOVE THEM, MESSERSCHMITTS GAVE THEIR PROTECTION...

Achtung! English fighters in the sun!

My God! There's even more now!

Jack! Look out behind you!

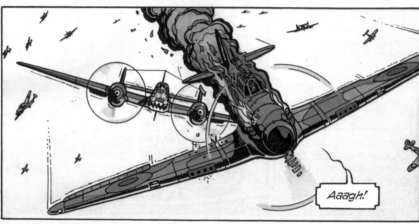

Aaagh!

ON THAT DAY, THE GERMAN ASSAULT WAS STOPPED, COSTING 34 BRITISH FIGHTERS...

ON THE 18ᵀᴴ OF AUGUST, THE ENGLISH LOST 27 PLANES TO THE GERMANS' 71. THE STUKAS DROPPED LIKE FLIES!

ON THE 20ᵀᴴ OF AUGUST, WINSTON CHURCHILL PAID HOMAGE TO THE PILOTS' COURAGE...

... Never in the field of human conflict was so much owed by so many to so few.

13

IN CAFFIERS, FRANCE, AT III/J.G.26, MAJOR GALLAND CAME DOWN TO LAND. THE SECOND PHASE OF THE BATTLE OF BRITAIN WAS ABOUT TO BEGIN. IT WOULD LAST FROM THE 18TH OF AUGUST TO THE 15TH OF SEPTEMBER. THE FIRST COST 175 BRITISH PLANES, 403 GERMAN...

VETERAN OF THE CONDOR LEGION, ADOLF GALLAND WAS APPOINTED BY GOERING AS COMMANDANT OF THE 26TH FIGHTER SQUADRON ON THE 18TH OF AUGUST. HIS FRIEND MÖLDERS WAS PUT AT THE HEAD OF THE 51ST. GALLAND WAS 28 YEARS OLD AND HAD SHOT DOWN OVER 35 PLANES...

We'll never make it! With 90 minutes of flight time, we only have 20 minutes for the mission!

What's more, the English are using their planes sparingly; we can't engage them in a frontal battle!

It must also be said that the downed English pilots land on their own territory and return to combat. Ours are made prisoners...

And we are flying on sight; the English have radars!

I said jokingly to Goering that I wanted a unit full of Spitfires! But we also need quad-motor bombers—our bi-motors are being sent to the slaughter...

Bring in Hauptmann Werner!

Hauptmann?*

*CAPTAIN

He has just been promoted to this rank and assigned to our squadron. He should be here tonight for the meeting with General Osterkamp.

IN THE GENERAL QUARTERS OF JADG2, WISSANT...

EIN FÜHRER

The Stuka that are too slow and vulnerable will be pulled out of operations. The attacks will be concentrated on the airfields of southern England.

The fighters will systematically escort the bombers and we'll make sure that there are no more missed meetings between the two!

Aah!

Mölders, mate, look at us, turned into delivery escorts!

The next massive attacks will take place on the 24th of August!

ON THE PLANNED DATE, THE HEINKEL 111H'S MADE THEIR WAY TOWARDS THE ENGLISH AIRFIELDS...

THE BOMBING BEGAN...

... THE MACHINE GUNS FOLLOWED...

15

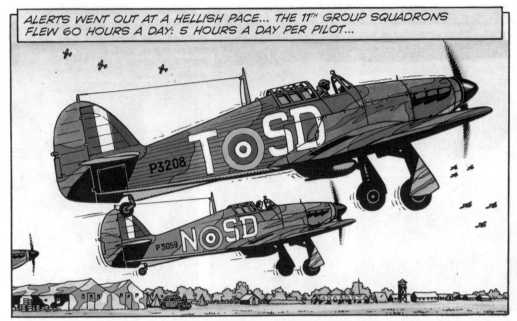

ALERTS WENT OUT AT A HELLISH PACE... THE 11TH GROUP SQUADRONS FLEW 60 HOURS A DAY: 5 HOURS A DAY PER PILOT...

JAMES H. COLBY ON THIS DAY...

This is Blue 1... My plane has been hit... No way to engage landing gear... I'm going to belly-flop!

Are you hurt, Sir?

I'll be all right...

Henry! Eggs and bacon are eaten with a fork, not with your nose!

?!!

We're all going to collapse!... Some of us are even sleeping in our planes... others have less than 10 hours of training!

AT FIGHTER COMMAND, THEY KNEW ABOUT THE DANGERS OF FATIGUE... BUT ANOTHER DANGER APPEARED...

Our recon planes have spotted concentrations of troops and landing craft in the Channel ports!...

Bomber Command has been informed. It has taken the necessary action...

INDEED, ON THE NIGHT OF THE 25TH OF AUGUST, THE ENGLISH BOMBED BERLIN...

AND THEN THE CHANNEL PORTS AND THE CALAIS PORTS WERE PILLAGED IN TURN...

Berlin bombed!'... There will be repercussions! What are my pilots doing?!

AND THE REPERCUSSIONS BEGAN. THE MOUTH OF THE THAMES WAS ABLAZE...

ON THE 31ST OF AUGUST, THE BIGGIN HILL AIRFIELD NEAR LONDON WAS BOMBED FOR THE FOURTH TIME IN TWO DAYS...

AMONGST THE PILOTS, MORALE WAS LOW...

Three more of our own hit the deck... It's a bloodbath!

YET, THE 4TH OF SEPTEMBER...

Mister Churchill is trying out his new discovery: night-time bombing! I've waited three months, but we'll fight fire with fire... We'll destroy their towns!

THE SECOND PHASE OF THE BATTLE WAS OVER. IT HAD COST 300 FIGHTERS, 103 PILOTS DEAD AND 128 INJURED ON THE ENGLISH SIDE. THE GERMANS HAD LOST OVER 400 PLANES...

ON THE 7TH SEPTEMBER 1940, AT CAP GRIS-NEZ, GOERING WAS THERE TO OVERSEE THE DEPARTURE OF THE FIRST RAID ON LONDON...

The raid will consist of 300 bombers protected by 600 fighters...

Good! Very good!

LONDON'S PORT BURNED...

THE ENGLISH FOUGHT BACK...

F. Bergèse

18

LEIGH-MALLORY BROKE THE RULE OF "SMALL PACKETS" AND LAUNCHED THREE SQUADRONS UNDER THE ORDERS OF DOUGLAS BADER...

DOUGLAS BADER, A 30-YEAR-OLD ACE WHO FLEW WITH TWO ARTIFICIAL LEGS, WAS ALREADY A GREAT HERO OF THE BATTLE OF BRITAIN. AGAINST THE "SMALL PACKETS" TACTIC, HE HAD BEEN ABLE TO CONVINCE THE CHIEF OF THE 12TH GROUP TO TAKE 60 FIGHTERS TO COMBAT IN ONE GO...

The Spits against the Messerschmitts, the Hurricanes against the bombers! *Tally ho!!!*

ON THAT DAY, THE GERMANS LOST 41 PLANES AND THE ENGLISH 28...

LATER...

Goering is doing us a favour! If the Germans had kept on bombing our airfields in the south, they would have been able to nail our last fighters!

MEANWHILE, NEW INTELLIGENCE SUGGESTED FURTHER LANDING ATTEMPTS...

Our land defences are non-existent. All the heavy material is still on the beaches in Dunkirk!...

The volunteers of the Home Guard only have pistols and old rifles! We have neither tanks nor cannons!...

19

We'll hit them over the heads with beer bottles, because that's about all we've got! Let's pray that this intel is wrong!

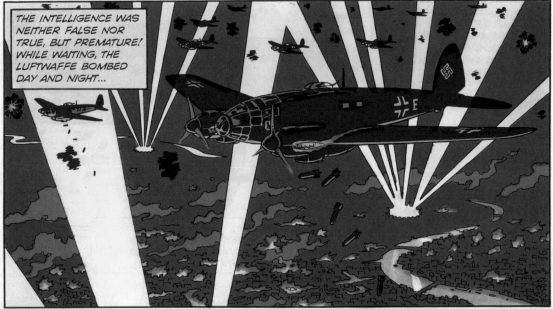

THE INTELLIGENCE WAS NEITHER FALSE NOR TRUE, BUT PREMATURE! WHILE WAITING, THE LUFTWAFFE BOMBED DAY AND NIGHT...

You won't get us!

FROM THE 1ST TO THE 10TH OF OCTOBER 1940, THE GERMANS LOST 107 PLANES...

It's unforgivable!... These bomber pilots are incompetent!!!

14TH OF NOVEMBER: COVENTRY
19TH OF NOVEMBER: BIRMINGHAM

ON THE 25TH OF NOVEMBER, A MEETING ATTENDED BY SIR PORTAL, CHIEF OF STAFF OF THE R.A.F., AND THE OTHER LEADERS OF THE AIR WAR...

This "small packets" technique is nonsense!

It's more economical to send 100 planes against 100 than 12 against 100!

Bader  Leigh-Mallory  Sholto Douglas  Sir Charles Portal

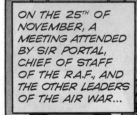

The results of my 12th group are proof!

We have to give up this policy of economic attacks!

SOME 24 HOURS LATER, DOWDING WAS DISMISSED AND REPLACED AT THE HEAD OF FIGHTER COMMAND BY SHOLTO DOUGLAS. KEITH PARK GAVE HIS PLACE TO LEIGH-MALLORY... HISTORY HAS A TENDENCY TO BE UNGRATEFUL TO THOSE WHO ARE RIGHT TOO SOON!

THE NIGHT BATTLES CONTINUED, DEFENCE RELYING PARTICULARLY ON THE HURRICANES AND DEFIANTS...

Boulton-Paul "Defiant"

ON THE 29TH OF DECEMBER, LONDON WAS BURNING. IN JANUARY AND FEBRUARY, THE ENGLISH PORTS SUSTAINED MASSIVE RAIDS...

MAY 1941, COLBY, NOW SQUADRON LEADER...

Look out behind you!...

Where?!

Bloody hell!!!

THAT MOMENT, COMMODORE GALLAND...

Reichsmarshal Goering is having a meeting in Paris for the heads of all units stationed in France...

21

THE FOLLOWING DAY, IN PARIS, GALLAND AND MÖLDERS MET...

This battle is bleeding us dry... A third of our bombers and a quarter of our fighters have gone down!

It seems that this conference is an invitation to continue the airborne war!

All that is just showing off, my friends!... After our victories in the Balkans and in Crete, the Führer has decided to attack the USSR!

Start a war on two fronts?

We'll shoot down the Russian pilots like rabbits!

The Luftflotte is heading east... Mölder's Squadron 51 will accompany. Yours will stay to contain the English!

Attack the USSR with a tired-out Luftwaffe!

We'll head straight back to England afterwards!

THAT NIGHT, COLBY GOT A VISIT FROM HIS BROTHER...

My arm will remain paralysed...

I learnt that you were appointed Chief of Staff for Bomber Command!

Yes, I can't wait to get out of this bed... Time for some return fire!

THE BATTLE OF BRITAIN NOW OVER, THE WAR STARTED IN THE EAST, BUT IT WASN'T YET TIME FOR GERMAN DEFEAT. THANK'S TO THE COURAGE OF A FEW AND TO THE TACTICAL GENIUS OF A MISUNDERSTOOD SIR DOWDING, HITLER WASN'T ABLE TO WIPE OUT GREAT BRITAIN... WHO KNOWS WHAT WOULD HAVE HAPPENED IF A FEW HUNDRED MEN HADN'T MADE THE SACRIFICE OF THEIR LIVES TO DEFEND THEIR COUNTRY?...

Francis Bergèse 6·83

22

# THE BOMBING OF GERMANY (1943 – 1945)

Three planes are missing... Ah! There's one!... His landing gear isn't out properly!

Fire!!! Everybody out! Quick!

?!!

Are you all right?

The gunner couldn't get out! He was hurt... I couldn't...

It could have happened to any of us!...

Hello, William! What a day!

Hello, Dave! So, the Americans made it in the end?!

We couldn't let you beat Adolf on your own!

Some cousins you are! How's my uncle Phil?

He's hiding his fear by shouting out these awful "Tally ho's"!

Have you been assigned to the 8th U.S.A.A.F.?

I fly a B-17. We're flying our first mission in three days.

See you after the debriefing!

ENCE CER

Colby?

The TI bombs lit our target well. The flak* was terrible, but I think I hit the goal!...

We went through a real wall of flak. Steven's plane blew up in front of me!

The German night fighters are getting aggressive!

*ANTI-AIRCRAFT GUNFIRE

SOON AFTER...

So, Steve, are you joining the hunt?

We've been training in Thunderbolts, but our scope for action is limited...

Alas! Our Spits don't go as far as Brussels. We are left alone over Germany at night...

Don't complain! We bomb by day and we're up against the Focke-Wulf 190!

2

Let's drink and let James get on with it!

Is your brother still with Bomber Command?

AIR CHIEF MARSHAL HARRIS. BOMBER COMMAND...

Our losses, which were 4.1% in 1942, are down to 3.6% now. But the night time bombing campaign is getting stronger... Over to you, Colby.

General Kammhuber's line, through his network of radars and fighters, stretches from the Netherlands, Denmark, and Westphalia to Hanover and the Ruhr... Our teams are sustaining attacks on the way there and back. Above the targets, there's flak...

We have to keep hitting German towns to destroy the population's morale!

The Americans who work during the day have asked us to take out their aeronautical industries.

Absolutely not! We have to annihilate the German towns!

JUNE 1943

The Point Blank Directive of the Joint Planning Team* asks the Americans to destroy the aviation factories.

As for us, we have to concentrate our efforts on industry.

* COOPERATION AND PLANNING COMMITTEE

Let the Americans do what they want! On the 31st of May 1942, with 1000 bombers, we destroyed Cologne. Tomorrow it'll be Hamburg!

THE 24TH OF JULY 1943, 23:00 HOURS...

We have to meet up with the Halifaxes* in nine minutes, then head for Lübeck and Hamburg!

There'll be more than 700 of us over Hamburg!

* ANOTHER MODEL OF BRITISH FOUR-ENGINED BOMBER

LATER, AN IMMENSE FLOTILLA OF BOMBERS WAS HEADED FOR GERMANY UNDER THE COVER OF DARKNESS...

It's a walk in the park! The Germans haven't moved a muscle!

We blinded their radar coverage by dropping strips of tin!

Hamburg! The P.F.F.* have dropped their flare bombs! Get ready!

* PATH FINDER FORCE

Home time!

THE BOMBING CONTINUED INTO THE NIGHT OF THE 27TH JULY, AND ON THE 2ND AND 3RD OF AUGUST 1943. IN FOUR NIGHTS, 2630 BOMBERS DROPPED 8261 TONNES OF BOMBS, HALF OF THEM PHOSPHOROUS.

THE LUFTWAFFEN-BEFEHLSHA-BERMITTE, RESPONSIBLE FOR THE DEFENCE OF THE REICH...

All of our emergency services were pulverised. The phosphorus set off storms of flame... temperatures reaching 1000°C...

It's unimaginable!

OF WHICH GOEBBELS WROTE:

A catastrophe that defies imagination!

We have to reorganise our night and day air defences. Bring back the planes from the Eastern front!

AS FOR OTTO WERNER...

They're getting us back for the Battle of Britain... It will be hard. I accept Galland's proposition: I'll join the night fight!...

IN THE GENERAL QUARTERS OF THE R.A.F...

We'll continue our strategic bombing... The German population will beg for mercy!

The Americans don't share our opinion. They're focus-sing their efforts on ball-bearing factories!...

James, the Air Chief Marshal has assigned you to the 8th U.S.A.A.F. as liaison officer!...

OCTOBER 1943...

James! Great to see you!... Think of me when I'm over Germany!

I'll do my best, Dave! Will I see you tonight?

Wing Commander Colby!

Welcome!... We have a meeting tomorrow morning at 6:00 hours. I'll show you your office!

THE FOLLOWING MORNING...

After this presentation of the situation, I'll hand you over to General Spaatz.

Since our raid on Schweinfurt, our losses have been substantial... Moreover, the factory is practically back to its former production levels!

On the 14th of October, P47s, thanks to an additional fuel tank, will be able to accompany the B-17s on Mission 115 up to this line. A relief force will come to meet them to assure their safe passage home...

RAF
8th USAAF
9th USAAF

Hambourg
Hanovre • Berlin
Ruhr Leipzig
Cologne • Dresden
Brussels Bonn
Frankfurt • Schweinfurt
• Ratisbonne

Thunderball line of action

14TH OF OCTOBER 1943...

It's a family mission! My brother Steve is flying a P-47 escort... He'll meet us when we get back.

Fighter alert! Strong concentration of bombers and fighters!...

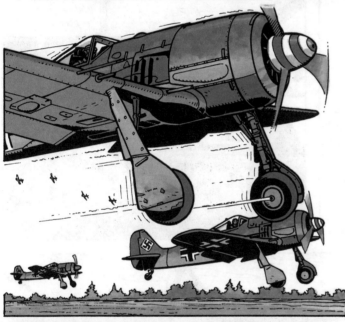

WHILE THE FOCKE-WULF 190S TRIED TO KEEP THE THUNDERBOLT ESCORT DISTRACTED, A MASS OF ALL KINDS OF MESSERSCHMITTS ATTACKED THE BOMBERS...

Try to avoid the Fockes! Go for the Messerschmitts!

Bandits at 3 o'clock! Shoot! Shoot!

That's all I'm doing! I got him!!!

That's Slim's plane!... What's it going to be like after Aix, when the P-47s can no longer follow?

Fuel up quickly! Their fighters have gone. They're ours now!!!

Oh, Lord! Flak now... Hold on tight!

We're approaching the target...

Bombs away!

8

MEANWHILE...

Let's go and protect Dave's return journey!

Damn it! Smoke... We may miss them!

INDEED, THE ESCORT PLANES NEVER MADE IT IN TIME TO JOIN UP WITH THE B-17S...

I can't control her anymore! Time to parachute!... Jump!

ON THAT DAY, 60 B-17 "FLYING FORTRESSES" WERE SHOT DOWN, FIVE TAKEN OUT ON THE RETURN JOURNEY, 12 MADE IT BACK TOO DAMAGED TO USE AND 121 WOULD HAVE TO BE REPAIRED...

The Americans suffered more than 20% losses... One of my cousins disappeared...

General Spaatz is fighting in vain... The American raids are not efficient!

The Germans have spread out and put their factories underground... They are producing more planes than before! We have to keep bombing their towns... Target: Berlin!

THE END OF 1943. THE NEW HEINKEL HE219S ARE EQUIPPED WITH LICHTENSTEIN RADARS FOR NIGHT BATTLES...

Berlin is still on fire!...

There were over 400 bombers!

You got a Halifax, Eric! Nice shot!

35th victory! I'll see you in the meeting room, Otto!... General Galland is visiting us.

We'll give back hit for hit. Every raid costs them 50 bombers. We're producing 1000 planes a month and we have synthetic fuel...

... But we have to concentrate 70% of our people on the west... Our soldiers need air cover in the east!

10

We'll have new weaponry... The Messerschmitt 109 G-6 is already equipped with a cannon capable of shooting 600 shots a minute, and we're preparing a revolutionary airplane!

30TH OF MARCH 1944...

Quickly! Get in the cockpit, Karl! They're attacking Nuremburg!

ON THAT NIGHT, EVERY PLANE THE GERMAN AIR FORCE HAD AVAILABLE TOOK OFF FOR A DOGFIGHT WITH THE BRITISH BOMBERS...

Bombers at 11 o'clock!

Got 'em!

Our radar is great!...

They haven't seen me. The wakeup call will be brutal!

*DEVIL!

*Teufel!/*

I thought that we'd had it then!

Below the Lancasters!

I'll take the leader!

I didn't get him... Let's go back!

Look! At 10 o'clock... Another Fritz has taken one of us out!

Look out!!! He's coming back... At 8 o'clock!

!?!

THAT MORNING, AT BOMBER COMMAND...

Oh, God!

Something wrong, James?

My brother was shot down over Nuremburg!

It was a real massacre... Hundreds of bombers taken to ground... Nearly 14% losses!

AT THE 8TH U.S.A.A.F. GENERAL QUARTERS, GENERAL SPAATZ...

The English were demolished... It was their turn! But our worries are behind us... With the P-51 we'll be able to accompany our bombers to the heart of Germany.

NORTH AMERICAN P-51 MUSTANG. 2000KM FLYING RANGE WITH EXPANDABLE FUEL TANKS. 700KM/H. 6 X 12.7MM CALIBRE BROWNING MACHINE GUNS.

FoBergèse 13

I can't wait to fly over Germany in that!... Right, see you tomorrow... I'm going out tonight!

THAT NIGHT...

Hello, James!

Christine, my fiancée... Laura, a friend... Take a seat! This place is quiet... Well, for as long as the V1s leave it in peace!

Be quiet! There's no point in calling them!

So, you like your Mustang, Steve?

We're going on a mission in two days... Bomber escort over the sorting station... But tonight, let's forget it all!

V-1 alert!... Take cover!!!

BRROOM!

There wasn't enough time to get down!

AFTER THE ALERT...

I hope that you'll make them pay for what they've done!...

You can count on me!

14

MAY 1944... THE ALLIES HAD DESTROYED THE COMMUNICATIONS PATHWAYS TO DISRUPT THE INVASION PLANS...

They're demolishing the rail stations and the refineries!

Let's go back. I'm nearly out of fuel...

Mosquito behind! Aargh!...

I'll get him over the airfield flak!

Phew! That was close... He nearly turned us into a sieve!

The front wheel won't come out...

Major Werner will be all right... but Karl is still in there.

AUGUST 1944... We're in ruins... The Americans won the Battle of Normandy and Paris has been retaken!

We won't have a front line radar detection network soon either... It's in the hands of the enemy.

Galland thinks that our daytime dogfighting has lost over a thousand planes... Setz, Hanning, Lemke, Mayer, Ubban, Oesau... All shot down!

... Galland's brother... But Novotny is still with us: over 200 victories!

You'll fly with him soon! He'll take you as his second in his ultra-fast fighting squad in a Messerschmitt 262!

To think that that jet plane has flown since 1941 and that our leaders doubted it!

A FEW MONTHS LATER, THE ACE NOVOTNY WAS SHOT DOWN TOO... DECEMBER 1944...

Targets straight ahead! Let's go!!!

SPITTING FIRE FROM ALL THEIR CANNONS, THE JETS SPED RIGHT INTO THE MIDDLE OF THE B-17 FORMATION...

AND GOT AWAY EVEN BEFORE THE PROTECTION FIGHTERS HAD TIME TO INTERVENE...

Another notch on the post!

Of course, it reaches 800km/h, but its range is only 1000km...

Our troops have launched an offensive in the Ardennes... The Americans are trapped!

But they don't have any air cover left!

INDEED, STEVE, WHO WAS NOW FLYING IN THE LATEST VERSION OF THE MUSTANG, THE P-51D...

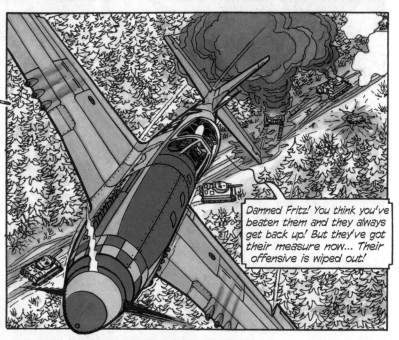

Damned Fritz! You think you've beaten them and they always get back up! But they've got their measure now... Their offensive is wiped out!

Look! Typhoons... They'll finish the job! The Germans are done for.

NOT QUITE... THE 1ST OF JANUARY 1945, THE LUFTWAFFE LAUNCHED OPERATION BODENPLATTE...

IT WAS THE LAST ROLL OF THE DICE FOR GERMAN AVIATION. SOME 900 FIGHTERS ATTACKED THE COMPLACENT ALLIES' AIRFIELDS AT 9:20AM. MORE THAN 350 PLANES WERE DESTROYED OR DAMAGED ON THE GROUND. THE GERMANS LOST 215 PILOTS...

14TH FEBRUARY 1945... After the English, the Americans took it out on Dresden! There are already tens of thousands of burn victims from the phosphorus...

Mein Gott! Dresden was just declared an open city too!

F. Bergèse

18

44

BUT THIS TIME, THE ESCORT FIGHTERS REACTED QUICKLY...

Today I'll show these 262s what flying is!

Red 1 to all... Leave the leader to me!

With only one jet engine left, I can't shake him... I have to get back to base...

The flak... Try not to hang around here too long!...

I'm as injured as my poor plane... The strip... The sun... One last time...

45

Look at that victory roll!

Yes, it's Steve... He got his 262!

758

Oberstleutnant Werner was shot down...

Novotny... Werner... It's the end... We have to see this through!

3RD OF MAY 1945, SALZBURG AIRFIELD...

They're not even attacking... They want to keep our ME 262s intact!

Tanks are rolling into Salzburg!

Burn the planes!

Jawohl, Herr General!

LONDON...

Peace! ... Peace!...

It's over! Peace is here! Long live the R.A.F.!

Yes... Peace is here...

THE EUROPEAN BOMBINGS WOULD COST THE ALLIES 158,000 KILLED, IMPRISONED OR DISAPPEARED, 21,917 BOMBERS AND 80 BILLION 1945 DOLLARS. SOME 410,000 GERMAN CIVILIANS WERE KILLED. AT THE END OF THE WAR, DESPITE THE SCALE OF THE DAMAGE CAUSED BY THE ALLIES, THE REICH'S FACTORIES PRODUCED MORE PLANES THAN THEY DID IN 1940.

Francis Bergèse 08.83

## "WHEN WE NEEDED TO GET AWAY FROM IT ALL RAFA GAVE US A BREAK"

The Royal Air Forces Association is here to offer friendship, help and support to today's RAF family in their times of need. From those who have served to those who serve now.

In this case we were able to offer the family of an ex-serviceman, who now suffers from Huntingdons, a much needed break at one of our respite homes.

But this is just the tip of the iceberg.
In a typical year our Welfare Officers will make around 25,000 visits. We will organise over 3,000 respite care breaks at our homes.
We will be there to provide war pension and AFCS advice and representation, do home and hospital visits and provide support for families whenever it's needed.

As a charity, we rely on membership fees and donations to enable us to continue this vital work. So if you'd like to join, help out or make a donation please contact us via any of the methods below. Many, many thanks.

Membership: www.rafa.org.uk
Donations: www.wingsappeal.org.uk
Telephone for either: 0116 266 5224
Or if you'd prefer to write:
The RAF Association,
117¹/₂ Loughborough Road, Leicester LE4 5ND.

*Be part of something special*

**◎ ROYAL AIR FORCES Association**

Friendship | Help | Support

Registered Charity 226686 in England & Wales. SC037673 in Scotland